Where are the Men?

A Study of an Endangered Species

by

Gavin Wakefield

Assistant Curate, Anston, Sheffield

gb GROVE BOOKS LIMITED

Bramcote   Nottingham   NG9 3DS

CONTENTS

THE COVER PICTURE

is by Peter Ashton

INTRODUCTION

We need more women. More women counsellors over there. Not the plea of this booklet, but the call night after night at Mission England in Sheffield 1985. That spurred me to consider the reasons for the greater numbers of women than men in English churches.

Presented here is a brief statistical survey and an outline of the reasons suggested for the imbalance. It is followed by a strategy for countering the trend, taking up ideas which are known to have worked. This involves teaching Christian men as well as evangelizing non-Christian men. Both are necessary: to hearten those already Christians and to show non-Christians what discipleship means.

It does not claim to set out a fool-proof method for seeing men converted. Indeed, we ought to be suspicious of any such claim. What it should help you to do is to ask some of the right questions and learn about some of the answers being given by other churches.

ACKNOWLEDGEMENTS

Thanks go to many people who have contributed to the ideas expressed here. In particular I must thank Bill Howe, Gordon Oliver and Fran Wakefield—they may not agree with it all but have helped me considerably. Peter Ashton contributed the cover picture, and Pem Stratford has been a marvellous typist—thank you.

First Edition June 1988

ISSN 0144-171X

ISBN 1 85174 085 6

1. SURVEYING THE SCENE

'On the far flung field of battle
In the bivouac of life
You will find the Christian soldier
Represented by his wife.'

The contemporary debate on the roles of women and men has understandably concentrated on questions of leadership and power. That most churches operate with a male hierarchy is not in doubt, but this has tended to obscure the fact that in a typical English congregation there are likely to be twice as many women as men. The concern of this first chapter is to clarify and sharpen that picture for us.

It would be helpful if we could have a full historical and global perspective, but that is hard to obtain. Questions of membership definitions, problems in surveying congregations and tension over interpretation of the results all remain. I have it on good authority that there are no data kept on the ratio of men to women worldwide.[1] What follows in this chapter is an attempt to give some background and perspective to our thinking.

1 The Modern Era

We begin with a few comments from other parts of the world: for example, in Latin America Roman Catholicism is often seen as a religion for the rich and the women.[2] In South Africa studies of independent black churches have found typically that two-thirds of the adherents are women,[3] and they have a status higher than in the traditional tribal society.

In India in the 1920s and 30s a similar raising of women's status was found.[4] These examples seem to provide a comparison with the first century Mediterranean world: in all cases the coming of Christianity raised the status of women, and so it is plausible, though not proven, to assume that women would belong to the church in greater numbers than men.

More details are available from the U.S.A. A collection of various measures indicates the preponderance of women over men in American churches, though not in as pronounced a way as in Britain.[5] There are reported differences between denominations. Catholic and Orthodox churches have more equal numbers of men and women, and as one moves to more 'extreme' Protestant groups the ratio of women to men gets higher. However, the figures do need to be treated with some caution since there seem to be differences in the way membership is counted. One final piece of interesting evidence comes not from Christianity but Judaism: in the first generations of immigrant Jews the men are more pious and

[1] C. Wagner, private communication 18 December 1985.
[2] Survey of Chilean working men, 1963, in E. Norman *Christianity in the Southern Hemisphere* (1981), p.39.
[3] *Op. cit.,* p.158.
[4] J. W. Pickett *Christ's Way to India's Heart* (1938), pp.86-8.
[5] M. Argyle and B. Beit-Hallahmi, *The Social Psychology of Religion* (1975²) chapter 5.

traditional in belief, but then the women begin to predominate. The implication is that it is not something inherent in the religious belief system but a cultural pressure which causes this.[1]

2 The English experience
(i) Historically
The earliest figures of use come from the end of the nineteenth century when confirmation figures are available for the Church of England. It is also reported that the 'preponderance of women in English churches was first noted in the 1890s and corroborative evidence comes from the experience of chaplains in the First World War.[2] They found that working men were generally not in touch with the churches, those in touch being no more than 20% of all men.[3] Furthermore, what religion they had was informed almost solely by Sunday School education and not adult worship. However the rot did not set in because of the war as is often thought:

> 'The war revealed the extent of the alienation of the majority of the English male population from the life and practices of the churches— it revealed it, it deepened it, but it certainly did not create it.'[4]

It seems that the earlier experience of the Industrial Revolution and the associated social upheaval is more to blame.

(ii) Trends in belonging
To give some perspective to the figures that follow it is worth noting that the 1981 census found a female/male ratio of 1.09:1[5] in the adult population (16+). This figure does not change rapidly. So the idea that churches have more women as members because there are more women only accounts for a small part of the observed differences, as we shall see below. Indeed, men now outnumber women in all age groups under 50.

A couple of surveys suggest that there may be denominational differences in England. At churches in the city of York in 1951 the following female/male ratios were found for church attendance:[6]

Non-conformist 1.57: Church of England 1.48: Roman Catholic 1.23

The Nationwide Initiative in Evangelism found in the late 1970s the following ratios:

Methodist 2.2: Church of England 1.6: Roman Catholic 1.4

[1] D. R. Hoge and D. A. Roozen (ed.) *Understanding Church Growth and Decline 1950-1978* (1979), p.43.
[2] Argyle and Beit-Hallahmi, p.73. Unfortunately they give no source for this statement.
[3] A. Wilkinson *The Church of England and the First World War*, p.163.
[4] *Ibid.*, p.7.
[5] This type of ratio is subsequently written simply as 1.09. I make use of ratios rather than percentages for two reasons; the first is that ratios show up changes more easily; the second is more subjective, it is easier to picture a group in which there are 2 women to 1 man, than where 33% are men. A ratio of 1 means equal numbers of men and women, ratios less than 1 mean more men, ratios higher than 1 mean more women.
[6] Argyle and Beit-Hallahmi, p.76.

More recently, *Faith in the City* reported a ratio of 1.7 in the Church of England.[1] A MARPLAN poll in November 1986 produced a ratio of 1.6 for reported weekly attendance at a church.[1] What the figures show clearly is the undoubted preponderance of women in churches and what they suggest is that the situation may be getting more imbalanced.

The imbalance is highlighted in Church of England confirmation figures. The interpretation of these over the last century is not entirely straightforward but I make an attempt.

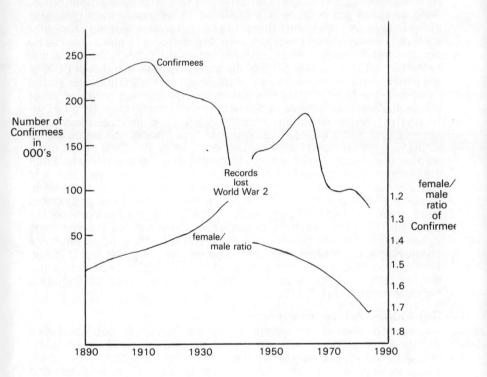

The diagram is a simplified description of the number of confirmations and the female/male ratio of candidates.[3] It is clear that the total number of candidates has declined since about 1960 and faster than the birth-rate has fallen. Until the 1970s virtually all candidates were teenagers. The

[1] *Faith in the City*, p.36, para. 2.35.
[2] Reported in *Church Times*, 12 December 1986.
[3] All the figures are calculated from the tables published by the Central Board of Finance of the Church of England.

experience prior to the Second World War suggests an improving balance between boy and girl candidates, something broken after that war. Since the 1970s the number of adults being confirmed is rising substantially and in 1984 was approximately one-third of the total. In other words, the pattern is increasingly one of fewer confirmees, adult confirmees and female confirmees. As the total number has gone down so the *proportion* which is male has fallen markedly.

When individual dioceses are compared great variations show up. For example, some southern ones such as Salisbury and Oxford regularly have lower female/male ratios for confirmees, where some northern ones such as Newcastle, Durham and Sheffield regularly have higher ratios. Because I work in the Diocese of Sheffield, I have looked more closely at these figures and the trends there do seem to contain pointers for other parts of England. When the figures are broken down by age as well as by sex, the trend towards adult confirmation as the norm is very obvious. Indeed by 1985 well over 50% of the male confirmees and over 60% of the female confirmees were aged 16 and over, mostly 20 and over. At the same time the female/male ratio increases with the age group. In other words, the adult confirmees, which are surely correctly thought to be better on the grounds of a mature commitment, are even more likely to be females than in the younger age-groups.[1] This finding was borne out by similar figures obtained for Derby Diocese. The implications of this trend are that the church is increasingly attracting adult women only and that the number of adult men will diminish. It also means that work amongst teenage boys is of increasing importance. Attention has been drawn to this by the Bishop of Sheffield.[2] Obviously the situation in other dioceses needs to be checked but I suggest that such figures point to a prospect of a Church of England run by men almost solely for women in some areas unless the trends can be altered. Finally, lest it be thought that this is a purely Anglican problem, the earlier figures given suggest that it is not. Furthermore, the interdenominational Mission England rallies found a similar pattern of response, with the female/male ratio of enquirers typically in the range 1.7-1.8.

(iii) Individual Congregations
Surveys of individual congregations have not been widely published even though it is through that means that people are generally joined to the church universal. One good source was the Urban Church Project[3] which made surveys in the late '70's and early '80's. The Anglican and Methodist churches surveyed all had female/male membership ratios in the range 1.4-2.0, and so are fairly typical of the vast majority of English congregations in that respect House churches with which I have checked are in the range of 1.25 to 1.5. One particular finding made by Wasdell[4] and confirmed at least in part by my own investigations is the connection between a growing church and the female/male ratio of converts. Where

[1] If a reader is interested in analyzing detailed figures, the Diocesan or Bishop's Office should be able to supply them, not the Central Board of Finance.
[2] Response to Articles of Enquiry, 1982, p.6.
[3] Papers available from David Wasdell, St. Mathias Vicarage, Poplar High Street, London E14 0AE.
[4] D. Wasdell *Tools for the Task No. 1*, p.36.

a church is growing in numbers this ratio gets closer to one, whereas in a church which is steady or falling in numbers the ratio becomes imbalanced, often reaching five new women to every new man. It must be noted that this applies to conversion growth rather than those transferring from other congregations. Furthermore, the application to a congregation must not be made on a snap-shot basis, but must be dynamic, looking at the trends within the congregation over a period of years. More is said on this in Chapter 3, with regard both to surveying the congregation and planning for growth. This finding seems to be reflected on the large scale by the Church of England confirmation figures already referred to.

3 Looking Back

Detailed information from the past is harder to find and differences in culture must be taken into account. However, we can learn something from the concerns of Christians in the past.

(i) The New Testament

Jesus attracted men, taught men, gave men responsibility, changed men. He did the same for women and that has its own significance. We need to remember that Jesus in his earthly ministry drew men to himself. We do not know how many men and women followed him. That was not important. What counted was following and being changed.

As the story of the church is unfolded in the Acts of the Apostles we find changes from Jewish practice with men admitting women to their prayer meetings (1 v 14). On the day of Pentecost the Holy Spirit was poured out on men and women (2.17ff). We find the good news appealed to men and women, suggesting an openness to women unusual in other current religions.

The openness to women led to tension between church fellowship and social conventions. We see evidence of that in the Epistles. It is possible that the good news appealed more to Gentiles, slaves and women rather than their counterparts because they had most to gain from equality. This may be supported as far as gender is concerned by 1 Peter 3.1-7. Wives may well have unbelieving husbands (v.1) while husbands are assumed to have believing wives.

In general, the Epistles are more concerned with gender roles, which we will look at in Chapter 3. The silence on the numbers of men and women may be taken in two ways. Perhaps we should not worry about numbers at all, simply on getting relationships ordered in a godly way. Alternatively, perhaps the New Testament churches were well-balanced between men and women. David Wasdell's thesis on growing churches might apply here, though it is impossible to be sure.

(ii) Later Centuries

In the early centuries of the church we know that men predominated in its leadership, though we do not know about the membership. It is also clear that women often played leading roles. For example, the conversion of a

7

husband through his wife's example, described in 1 Peter 3.1, is also found in Tertullian[1] and in the late fourth century *Apostolic Constitutions.*[2] Martyrdom of women made a deep impression on those who witnessed their faith. Celsus charged that Christianity only appealed to the lower classes, 'with women and children.'[3] In these examples we see expressions of the way in which 'Gentile, slave and female' responded to the liberating good news.[4]

However, as the church was 'nationalized' in the early fourth century, the basis of membership and affiliation changed and an increasing emphasis on the male hierarchy came into theological thinking. This means that it is men who are most obvious in large parts of church history. Their use of power was not always in accordance with the servant role taught by Jesus. But there were men able to provide inspiration to others: St. Benedict, St. Cuthbert, St. Francis of Assisi, John Wycliffe spring to mind. The importance of this for us is in giving different models of how men down the years have tried to follow Christ.

The Reformation brought about some changes in thinking about men and women. For example, Luther broke with the mediaeval suspicion of sex and began a great change of views on virginity, celibacy and marriage. Calvin even stressed the companionable side of marriage against the pro-creative.[5] Thus women gained in status somewhat, without having to remain perpetual virgins to achieve it. Nonetheless, there remained many ways in which men continued to dominate women, even in the church, a situation which prevails today. I refer to leadership rather than numbers, of course.

4 Summary

On the whole the church in England is failing to attract as many men as women in quite a pronounced way. There is some evidence that this has been a problem in the past, in this country and elsewhere. On the bright side there are growing churches which seem to have female/male ratios which are getting better. So far this has not been enough to reverse the overall trends but as more churches learn these lessons it is possible for us to see a reversal. Overall church growth and improving the female/male ratios seem to go hand-in-hand.

[1] *Ad Uxorem* 2.3-7.
[2] *Ap. Const.* 1.10.
[3] Origen, *Contra Celsum* 3.44.
[4] These and other comments can be found in M Green *Evangelism in the Early Church* (Highland Books 1984), pp.51 and 209-14.
[5] E. Storkey, *What's Right with Feminism*, p.138

2. WHY ARE THERE FEWER MEN?

'The weaker sex is the stronger sex because of the weakness of the stronger sex for the weaker sex.'

This saying is a reminder of the confusion in our thinking about gender roles. What follows is meant as a stimulus to your thinking, not the definitive answer.

The imbalance in male/female numbers in church congregations has not gone unnoticed by investigators from within and without the church. We all know that Christianity and the church is 'for women and children, not grown men—at least we do if we are on the outside. That impression is substantiated by the statistics in the previous chapter.

Here are the main reasons given by researchers in this field. The male/female differences described are related to our church organizations in the last section of this chapter.

1 Theological explanations

I know of no-one who suggests God wants to call more women than men! Indeed, in Christ there is no 'male and female' (Gal. 3.28) and on these grounds one would expect roughly equal numbers of men and women.

However, there are suggestions in popular books[1] and from some preachers that the church as a whole has given in to liberal, feminist ideas about gender roles and so lost men. The solution offered is a particular hierarchical model, usually based on the nuclear family.[2]

The exegesis given of key texts, such as Genesis 1-3 and 1 Corinthians 11.2-16, is open to criticism: Genesis 1.26f. applies equally to men and women; the subordination of women is a consequence of the Fall (Genesis 3.14-19); the argument that more liberal thinkers have read into the text their own disposition also applies to many others, of previous ages as well as this.[3] The evidence of the English statistics in Chapter 1 is also not favourable: the proportion of men in churches was relatively low even when traditional ideas were stronger.

More positively, the creation texts point us to man's dependence on God—a feature often stressed in churches and more appealing to women in our culture—and also to the authority and power given to humankind (Genesis 1.26-30). It is the imbalance in teaching here which is a likely theological factor leading to the female/male imbalance in church.

Further, the case for challenging men about following Christ is important and we will take it up later. To this extent there are theological explanations, which inter-act with the following ones.

[1] e.g. Elisabeth Elliot *The Mark of a Man*, p.81; the Dobson series of books.
[2] A widely sold example is Larry Christenson *The Christian Family* (Kingsway 1981).
[3] More details in Mary Hayter *The New Eve in Christ* (SPCK, 1987), Chapters 5-7; Storkey, *op. cit.*, pp.151-6.

2 'It's Built-in' explanations

How far the physical differences between men and women are reflected in psychological and spiritual differences has been much debated. It is made complicated by social conditioning which varies so much.

Animal studies are of some use, though human beings are more than 'naked apes'. But primates are our closest animal relations and it has been found that female primates are less aggressive and more fearful than males; they are also generally more submissive and passive.[1]

There are some differences which are not all in the mind, contrary to the beliefs of some of the more extreme feminists. These differences should not be exaggerated, since there is considerable overlap between the sexes, even in the areas described. Social conditioning plays a major role in shaping aggression or social competence. At a simple level contrast a downtrodden peasant with a successful salesman, both moulded by their social circumstances.

(i) Boys are in general more aggressive than girls

Two American researchers wanted to show that there were no real differences between the sexes: careful reviews in the whole literature of psychology forced them to recognize several real differences. The most important one is that boys really are more aggressive than girls.[2] Contrary to much popular belief boys are more aggressive than girls physically *and* verbally. The disruptive four-year old child in church is more likely to be a boy than a girl.

Many congregations are seen as passive and I suggest that it is *not* because they are largely made up of women, but *vice versa:* men are not so readily attracted to a passive experience. The Western version of Christianity emphasizes receptivity and passivity: this is sometimes related to the female role in childbearing, 'the soul is always female towards God'. This is not the case for all forms of religion, just one example being militant Islam, a very active religion of men.

(ii) Girls are in general more socially competent than boys[3]

Both sexes have similar overall self-confidence, but boys tend to crash through in an unknown social setting, where girls are better at picking up tacit cues and knowing what to do. 'Take your hat off' (or more likely cap!) hisses the missus to the ignorant hubbie going to church for a wedding or baptism. We can enhance this effect if the leader of a service or meeting takes no account of the needs of newcomers. On the whole, women prefer smaller groups, men much larger ones—the herd instinct.[4]

(iii) Women have more guilt feelings than men

This is a view expounded in the textbooks[5] and used to explain the greater proportion of women as we move from Catholicism to extreme Protestan-

---

[1] M. Argyle and B. Beit-Hallahmi *Social Psychology of Religion* (RKP, 1975[2]) p.77.
[2] E. E. Maccoby and C. N. Jacklin, *The Psychology of Sex Differences* (OUP, 1975) p.351.
[3] *op. cit.,* p.350.
[4] *ibid.,* p.349.
[5] e.g. Argyle and Beit-Hallahmi, *op. cit.,* p.77.

tism. I include it to warn against accepting too readily the views of social scientists. The Roman Catholic Church 'relies' as much as Protestant churches on guilt feelings. Does it mean that Protestant churches are more successful at helping women to cope with their guilt feelings or is the Roman Catholic Church more successful with men's guilt feelings?

Moreover, is it not more the case that there is a greater willingness on the part of women in our culture to admit to guilt feelings, and to emotions generally? Men usually cannot speak kindly of male colleagues' weaknesses, for example. Here we move into our next area of explanations.

3. Social and Cultural explanations

Most explanations by researchers are offered in this area. This reflects no doubt a widespread assumption that male/female differences are learnt and are not in-built. We have already seen some evidence that this is not entirely true. There is undoubtedly an interaction between biological, psychological and social factors in creating differences between men and women, but differences there always are.[1] However, the way in which our behaviour and beliefs can be moulded indicates the importance of social factors in considering church attendance. The factors described are essentially those to be found in our own society and age, though some apply cross-culturally. Of these four factors the first two are probably the more important ones.

(i) Differences in upbringing

In most societies, including our own in the recent past and still to a large extent today, girls are trained for 'nurturance, obedience and responsibility', boys for 'self-reliance and independence'.[2] This clearly relates to the different sex roles in child-bearing and rearing. It does not follow that women will then be more religious than men, that depends on the religion on offer and its presentation.

(ii) The separation of work and home

In our present society the English man and woman's home is his or her 'castle' to a previously unparallelled extent. Home and work have become more and more separated over the last 200 years. Those who go out to work usually live in (at least) two quite separate worlds, one public, one private, whatever the physical distance.[3] The parish system, based on residence, has failed to cope with the fragmentation of the lives of men in work.In the public world religion has been pushed to the periphery, often regarded as a nuisance and sometimes treated with hostility. In the private world, there is often confusion and difficulty in which women often give the lead and in which men often feel awkward. Even when women go out to paid employment they are far more likely to work in more personal environments, with their main contacts being other women; for example, nine out of ten infant and primary school teachers are women. Three out of four men work in segregated jobs, a higher proportion than at the start of the century.[4]

[1] M. Mead *Male and Female* (Penguin, 1962) p.31. This anthropologist makes it clear that sex roles are differentiated in all cultures, though not always in the same ways.
[2] M. Argyle and B. Beit-Hallahmi, *op. cit.,* p.77.
[3] L. Newbigin *Foolishness to the Greeks* (SPCK, 1986), especially pp.29-31.
[4] M. Langley, *Equal Women* (Marshalls, 1983) pp.152-4.

For many men (as well as increasing numbers of women) work provides security and an outlet. It is still largely true that men focus their lives around their work, and married women focus their's around their husband. This hits at both home and church: responsibilities there are left by default to wives. The dichotomy between the public and private worlds is the major factor but there are others, such as mental insecurity, uncertainty about male/female roles, new attitudes to sex, materialism, personal ambition, greed. This can be so for clergy as well, where it will hit the home and family first.

As a result of these arrangements and the biological roles, women tend to have a more person-centred view of life. Thus, 'I'd like the baby christened', is usually the mother's suggestion and she is the one who contacts the Vicar. The female link tends to be true for the other turning points of marriage and death.[1] It is noticeable that widows often become active members of churches after their husband's death.

Furthermore, without disparaging the work done by women at home, there is more opportunity for housewives to see the Vicar, even if it is in the company of a screaming baby. It does seem to be the case that women who go out to work tend to reduce their religious practice, whatever the exact details are by which this happens. It has to be acknowledged that most religious practices do require a certain amount of free time, probably more available to older women with children at school or without other heavy family commitments. The rather humdrum nature of these explanations must not blind us to their validity.

(iii) 'Men are less emotional than women'
This is one of those general statements which conceals its truth. It is easy to think of tremendous emotion expressed by men, whether it is as part of a football crowd with great noise or being vulnerable at a bereavement or getting angry over some trifling matter. What is true in our culture is that women find it easier to express emotions in intimate settings.[2] This has obvious implications for groups in which certain emotions are encouraged and explored. Others (anger in the PCC?) are not acceptable. It is seen in the greater willingness of women to seek prayer for healing: men are not usually 'allowed' to admit to weakness and need.

(iv) 'Men prefer the pub'
Of course, not all men like pubs but men do enjoy one another's company and will often join some group or another: suggestions include pigeon fanciers, darts teams, Freemasonry, London clubs and sports clubs. Women may belong to some of these groups but often a church provides an alternative fellowship to the men's beery fraternal. The church (usually) has plenty of women and will (again, usually) also provide a man who is solicitous and safe (called a minister, vicar, priest . . .).

[1] See the comment by M Silversides *Folk Religion: Friend or Foe?* (Grove Pastoral Series No. 25, 1986) p.8.
[2] E Storkey. 'So what's the difference?' in *Third Way* (Dec. 1985) p.24.

4. Factors in church organization

By now you will have already spotted several of these factors. This section is intended to highlight features in church life which promote a female/male imbalance. They are ordered roughly in line with the previous sections though naturally some relate to more than one explanation. Their consequences for our strategy are left to the next chapter.

(i) Passivity in church life

Much of our church life requires passivity and dependency, in the way we worship and meet generally. It is sometimes called 'wetness'. On the whole men prefer an active involvement or none at all. The amount of real responsibility and authority offered in most churches is very limited. Professional leaders remain wary of opening that up to others. The result is a stifling of initiative and especially for men, a weakening of the sense of belonging.

It is true of our worship. It is partly the way in which services are usually led: everyone dependent on one man at the front. Passivity often is reinforced in the content as well. Do some modern choruses give a rather effeminate impression? The general encouragement of boys to be independent and to look after themselves cuts across the dependency so often presented in church.

(ii) 'Boys are disruptive'

The greater restlessness of boys makes it harder to bring them into services where any disturbance is unwelcome. Even crches are not always able to cope. This brings about an imbalance at an early age. Even before the age of 7 far more girls than boys have been in church with parents.[1]

(iii) Strangeness of church ritual

To the outside man some things may appear 'wet' (see (i) above). Churches also do unexpected things—why does the choir turn round to say something (the Creed)?—and men can feel very awkward lest they do the wrong thing. This relates to the lower social competence of men. For some men the church feels very middle-class in its attitudes. It may not always be true, but it is a widespread perception and barrier.

(iv) The expectation of intimacy

Once a church begins to get beyond the 'religion is for the hour on Sunday' stage, men in our culture find it harder to be intimate and personal in their faith. Thus, home groups often accentuate the female/male imbalance, as we noted earlier.

(v) Children's work

Much of our work, especially that which is visible, relates to children, whether baptisms or Sunday school or even holiday clubs. This tends to reinforce the notion that church is basically for women and children. It is not helped if all the leaders of such work are women. Boys need good role models from Christian men in church, as well as in the home.

[1] J. and E. Newson *Perspectives on School at 7 years old* (Allen and Unwin 1977), p.100.

(vi) Clergy[1] visiting habits

Through pressure of evening meetings much visiting gets done in afternoons when it is more usually the wife of a married couple who is in. This is not always true when encountering shift workers or the unemployed, but it has been and remains a real factor. Where the woman is also out for paid employment the likelihood of a visit diminishes. Of itself visiting is unlikely to result in conversions anyway, but it remains an important link in maintaining membership.[2]

(vii) Clergy and Work

The jibe 'you only work one day a week' is not usually meant seriously but it indicates the ignorance of most people about what clergy do with their time. The ignorance is often there on both sides, for, although many clergy nowadays have work experience prior to ordination, it is usually of a professional kind. Furthermore, the experience of training and then parochial ministry tends to distance the clergy from the working lives of other men and women.

The difference in the setting of work is a major factor here. Most people in paid employment have a clear separation between home and work. For clergy this is not so. Whether desired or not, home and work and leisure become entwined. The advantage lies in the opportunity to integrate one's faith in all areas of life. A disadvantage is in forgetting the stresses and pressures in other jobs. The clergy in that respect are somewhat like housewives or active retired people.

(viii) Busy-ness of Christian men

These men already committed to Christ are often over committed to the church—in the sense that the lack of manpower leads them to be churchwarden, choirmaster and home group leader—all at once. In such a situation they become too busy for friendship with non-Christian men, even though friendship is important in conversion.

Women tend to have more intimate friendships, suited to the style of evangelism often used. Men generally have acquaintances and working friendships. In a society where religious faith is privatized, it is not done to be sharing it at work or even at leisure. Indeed, even home and church are often separated, so that the working out of discipleship is hard to see.

And finally

(ix) 'Imitate me as I imitate Christ'[3]

or, do we, as Christian men, provide a model worth emulating? This point is expanded in the next chapter but in essence it asks if we are truly disciples, followers after Christ or simply playing at religious games? For men to become disciples we need the simple and direct challenge of Christ: Follow me.[4]

---

[1] 'Clergy' is convenient shorthand here for full-time ministers of the church.
[2] Part of a plausibility structure of the faith, a term used by Peter Berger to describe social systems reinforcing a certain view of the world. It is most easily read up in *A Rumour of Angels*. Newbigin (*op. cit.*, pp.10ff.) also discusses this useful concept.
[3] 1 Cor. 11.1.
[4] Matt. 4.19; 8.22; 9.9; 16.24; John 12.26.

3. DEVELOPING A STRATEGY FOR THE CONGREGATION

In the previous chapters we have looked at the trends in church membership and at the reasons behind the imbalance between men and women in broad terms. Here we attempt to bring it to the level of the individual congregation, since that is the level at which we can have most effect. We usually see society changed only gradually but within a congregation change can happen far more quickly. My suggestion parallels the chapters of this booklet: past trends, present beliefs and teaching, and future possibilities. I take for granted in all this the need for prayer and seeking God's guidance through the Spirit.

1 The Past—Doing our Homework

The basic idea is to do for our parish or area what was done in Chapter 1 for England. That is to map out what has happened in this congregation in the past in the context of its immediate surroundings. If our congregation is in the midst of a retirement area it is likely to have a different profile from that of one by a university, and obviously more subtle variations exist. There are a number of measures which can be used, depending on the nature of the records kept.[1] The first is total membership, defined in the Church of England most readily as Electoral Roll membership. This has the advantage of being clear and is usually available. The main disadvantage is that, at least in the Church of England, different incumbents have varying views on the desirability of such rolls, some seeing them as status symbols to be kept high, others as liabilities which can bump up the quota! A record of changes of minister is therefore also necessary. A second measure is given by attendance at worship. Depending on the records kept this may refer to total numbers or to communicants. These can be sub-divided into two groups: the average Sunday congregation and the annual special occasions and festivals, which will show the size of fringe membership. Whichever measures are available and used, it is most helpful to display these visually on a graph. It is very unlikely that separate figures for men and women will be available but the purpose of this exercise is to compare any trends in total membership with the sex ratio of new members.

The next measure to examine is that of new members over the period covered by the graph already drawn. In the Church of England this is most appropriately given by confirmation figures, which should be found in the appropriate register. A decision has to be made about the age of confirmees. Reference was made in the national figures to trends in this area and it will probably be most helpful to consider the sex ratios of teenagers and adults separately. These ratios can also be plotted on the graph. There will inevitably be some fluctuations and it is trends we are interested in. If necessary the numbers can be averaged over 2- or 3-year periods. You will probably find that, if the graph of membership has been fairly level, the sex ratio of confirmees (or equivalent) is high, perhaps up to five women for every man. Where there has been sustained growth in numbers that ratio will have come down and perhaps become equal. This applies most clearly to convert numbers, not to those transferring from other churches.

[1] The relevant sections of *Tools for the Task* are very helpful in this area, going into more detail than is appropriate here. Also, *How Do Churches Grow?*, p.92f. and p.189f.

That observation, if it is accurate, does not of itself answer our desire for more converted men. What it does do is to point us to look at the pressures which restrict total congregational numbers. This is not in conflict with the observation of general social pressures noted in chapter 2. Rather, there is an interaction between social pressures of a widespread kind and the internal working of a congregation. If men and women are brought up with certain gender expectations there is little chance of keeping those out of church life. So men reared to be independent and leaders will not readily join a group where they are not independent or not leaders, or where they dislike the models on offer unless there are compensations. The same applies to women with similar self-concepts.

We can bring our picture as up-to-date as possible by a closer examination of the most recent Electoral Roll, or Membership List. From this we can find the current sex ratio of the congregation, likely to be in the range 1 to 2, but possibly higher still. Furthermore, we can draw up an age-sex profile by first estimating the age band of all the members, in 5- or 10-year groups. More detail is provided in books on church growth.[1] The age-sex pattern of a church acts like tree-rings, indicating points of growth and stagnation. Once the study is done it should clarify the roles and groups which help the men who do belong to stay. This exercise has prodded more than one church into action over their lack of men, usually by the starting of a men's group.

2 The Present—The Roles of Men

After all the preceding pages one could be forgiven for thinking that there are virtually no men left in the church but, of course, that is not the case and we must present some positive teaching to men. Given that this booklet is in a series mainly read by those in some kind of leadership, you, my reader, are most probably a man, quite independent of the subject matter. That raises the whole question of male hierarchy in the church, both clerically and among the laity. The further 'up' the scale one looks, the more men predominate; it is especially noticeable where it matters—in financial affairs. So the key issue is this: *do we challenge present cultural beliefs on gender roles or work within them?* Even that is a little too simple, because there is no longer *one* cultural belief on such roles. Different groups within society have very different expectations and we are divided by social class, education, religion, ethnic group and age.

In practice, therefore, we have to look at two poles: one is the Biblical perspective as we interpret it and the other is the group expectations within our area of work. It means asking if we are simply making our message relate to the culture, for example, by highlighting a strong masculine identity. Or are we betraying the essence of the gospel by our methods; for example, should an evangelist use *double entendre* jokes to get the congregation on his side?[2] When we have asked these sorts of questions we can begin to challenge or work with attitudes as most appropriate.

[1] e.g. *How Do Churches Grow?*, p.104f. and p.199; *Church Alive!*, pp.76-9.
[2] Paul had to face the dilemma more than once, e.g. Gal. 2, 1 Cor. 8-10, especially 10.31-3.

... (a) Why have men's groups?

There are two parts to this question, though the answers interlock.

(i) Why have groups for men only?
(ii) Why have groups for Christian men?

We need groups for men and for Christian men in particular for several reasons.

There has been a reaction against single-sex groups; to a large extent this is because of the stress on being the Body of Christ doing the same things together, and being the Family of God together.

The Church of England Men's Society has recently closed down, for example. House groups, which have benefitted many churches, are numerically dominated by women, often by as much as 3 or 4 to 1 man. Thus it is helpful to remind Christian men that they are not on their own. They have a peer group of fellow Christian men. The effect on a Christian man as well as a non-Christian man walking into a men-only group to learn about the Lord often shows on his face: amazement that other men should take Jesus so seriously. It is confronting the stereotypes that 'religion is for women and children', that Sunday School is run by old ladies and teenage girls, that men do not have emotional and spiritual needs. If your church cannot muster the numbers, think big! The diocese of Liverpool has held two meetings for men, with more than 1,000 attending. They are thinking about their next step.

Next we have to acknowledge the low level of spiritual maturity and expectancy of many men. Even in getting a group together you may be told 'It'll not work here'.

Women have often taken the lead in praying and spiritual growth and men need some space to do some catching up. Prayer for one another at work as well as at home broadens horizons. Being in groups where we cannot rely on the women to pray for us means we have to learn. Difficult, yes, but also worthwhile! In practical terms that may mean having a prayer breakfast on a regular basis—a leading evangelist finds these to be well-attended, even as early as 6 a.m.! What are the work patterns in your area? Is there an opportunity for a group in an afternoon, where men are unemployed or work particular shifts? Easier to arrange are prayer triplets: three men can find a time to meet for prayer. A challenge, yes, but possible.

A further use of men-only groups may be to discuss sexuality. That is not to say there are not occasions for couples to look at Christian principles together, but the particular pressures and temptations put on men in our society require men to be able to admit their weaknesses and needs in this area. Jim Smith's book *The Christian Man* is very realistic in beginning with this topic!

Finally, other men will begin to see Jesus more clearly as Christian men they know are transformed gradually into the likeness of Christ. One man I know has been challenged to consider Jesus seriously by watching, over a period of years, two men he knows well. His work colleague and a neighbour have themselves become disciples in that time and are being changed. That is what is challenging their non-Christian friend. So in taking time to encourage Christian men we are not wasting time better spent on evangelism. Rather, we are helping to equip the church in its task of mission.

. . . (b) What do we talk about?

When we get the men together what should be on our agenda? The diocesan meeting in Liverpool, mentioned before, went for talking about a demanding Jesus, one who looks for disciples prepared to count the cost. I would suggest that this is a good start. Whether it is men or women the cost of discipleship must be examined. A meeting specifically called for men needs to look in some detail at what discipleship means in daily life, as experienced by the men present.

Jim Smith's book *The Christian Man* is valuable for this very reason. He writes about personal, spiritual and family needs, about a man's work or lack of paid work, about leisure and being alone. One church took the second half of the Letter to the Ephesians as the basis for a weekend of practical teaching for men. Using this material here are some of the issues and questions we need to consider.

(i) Submission to Christ

In one sense this refers to our whole lives, but in a narrower sense it refers to the putting off of the old self—former habits and attitudes—and putting on the new, made to be like God (Eph. 4.22-24). So the direct question is 'Have you submitted to Christ in that way?' Here is the place to examine the cost of commitment, and the cost of continuous openness to God. It is taking up the cross and following Christ (Mark 8.34), an active, voluntary submission.[1]

Christian men also need challenging on attitudes. What does it mean to be 'completely humble and gentle' (Eph. 4.2)? Is it realistic in our society to advocate that for women, let alone men? Other points of conflict will occur to you: do you accept them or challenge them? Discuss prevailing cultural pressures and world views in order to give men a handle on thinking this through.

(ii) Submission to one another (Eph. 5.21)

This is a radical demand, at the heart of all the subsequent teaching. It cuts right across our society's assumption that men are independent (and that women need to be if they are not). To put it into practice challenges the way we are taught to think and behave. It means trusting God to be at work in our fellowship.

What does it mean to submit to one another within the church?

How do I come to the point of trusting God, even when I think others are wrong?

[1] This theme is developed in Richard Foster *Celebration of Disciple* (Hodder, 1980) chapter 8.

How does this apply to all the areas of my life?

(iii) Marriage, singleness and sexuality (Eph. 5.22-33)

Here are some of the questions that Christian men (and women) should face about their marriages or singleness:

Married: What does headship mean in our marriage?

In practical terms, what options are available to practise mutual submission or to be a servant husband?[1]

How do I express my love for my wife?

What are my responsibilities to my wife: materially, sexually, emotionally, spiritually?

Single: How do I cope with my state in a society which idolizes marriage?

How do I express my sexuality?

What are the positive aspects of being single?

Be sensitive in groups to any divorced and bereaved men, and also the homosexually orientated.[2]

(iv) Family Life (Eph. 6.1-4)

Most men at some stage will have to consider how to bring up children, and nearly all will face some questions over relating to parents. Again, helpful and thought-provoking material is available in the books mentioned. The issues to be raised include:

In our culture the home is often regarded as women's territory. How far is that a Christian idea?

What responsibility do I take for my children, materially, emotionally, spiritually?

How should family life be run, and priorities of time and money established?

What changes will the family go through as children get older?

What are my responsibilities to my parents, especially as they age?

Is the wider family important to me?

(v) Paid work and non-paid work (Eph. 6.5-9)

Two articles setting out a backcloth for a Christian perspective on work are 'Work, faith and freedom'[3] and 'What Place Does Work Have in God's Purpose?'[4] These are of value in giving a wider framework for our thinking about work and also supply further references. In brief, here are some of the questions we need to consider:

Why is work so important to us?

How can we see positive changes come about in working practices?

How should work and access to resources be linked?

[1] Compare *The Christian Man*, pp.83-103 and *What's Right with Feminism*, pp.169-173. Although they use different language there is a large degree of convergence between the two approaches in practice.

[2] There is useful material on sexual expression in Richard Foster, *Money, Sex and Power*, chapters 6-9.

[3] John W. Gladwin in *Themelios* Vol. 12, No. 3, p.88f.

[4] Graham Dow in *Anvil* Vol. 1, No. 2, pp.139-151. Available from 4 Priory Row, Coventry CV1 5EX.

Does God have a purpose in work: in general terms, in my particular job?

If married, have we considered the right working pattern for us, within the constraints of available work?

More personal questions are asked in Jim Smith's book.[1] These are the sort of personal issues we need to have in mind:

How do I behave in my work?

What is the difference between a gift and a bribe?

How do I treat others and how do they treat me?

What is permissible to keep the business going?

How do I get the best from work?

Some clergy spend time at work with men of their church: not to convert their colleagues but to understand their working environment. It may involve the pressure of travelling, being bored or embarrassed, or standing with a fellow Christian. Have you considered doing that?

(vi) Leisure

The New Testament makes no obvious comments about leisure. It is mostly a more modern concept, since we have more time and resources available to us.

Are my leisure activities appropriate for a Christian? (Watching blue movies?)

How do my leisure activities affect my other responsibilities in time, energy and in money? (Can I *really* afford to buy a hang-glider?)

In what ways can my leisure be a bridge to friendship with non-Christian men?

Are there ways in which my Christian discipleship is my leisure activity, seen only in relation to my 'spare' time?

(viii) Spirituality (Eph. 6.10-20)

Most kinds of spirituality on offer are very often seen in very passive terms, being receptive to God, open to the Holy Spirit, accepting what Christ has done for us. This is not wrong but for many men does not immediately appeal. For Christian men, challenging their culture, it is appropriate to learn this more passive side of spirituality. But it leaves the possibility of a more active spirituality, without trying to create spiritual Rambos.

Here are two pointers: the first is the recognition that spirituality is about the whole of our lives. How I treat other people, what activities I take part in is all spirituality. Making that more explicit may help men get past the first barrier of 'not doing anything'. Taking up one's cross is neither soft nor passive.

The second pointer comes from churches developing the Wimber model of healing ministry. They are finding that men are more likely to get involved with this style of prayer for healing than with others. The reason seems to be that men can contribute something in this way and are not required to be totally passive. It picks up the strand of authority inherent in the Genesis creation account.

[1] *op. cit.,* pp.116-138.

. . . (c) What do we do?

The issues I suggest we talk about should be on the agenda of the local church but they frequently slip between the cracks. Do many sermons on Christian attitudes to work say more than 'behave yourself and do as the boss says'? To tackle these subjects requires rethinking our church structures to some extent. A beginning can be made with one-off meetings or even a weekend aimed at men, but how can we go further? All the following suggestions have been found useful by one church or another.

(i) Topic Groups

A mid-week course on a specific topic, such as marriage or work or lifestyle, for a specific period of time. This requires a reasonable number willing to attend and might be a case for co-operation with another church. One course on marriage and the family was held separately for men and women.

(ii) Sport

Sports teams, catering for the need to relax in a Christian atmosphere. These include football, cricket, running, darts, snooker.

(iii) Prayer groups

A men's group. Successful ones often involve eating and/or drinking. Many churches have found a regular prayer breakfast of value. This can be on a small scale, involving mainly prayer for individuals. On a larger scale invited speakers can open up areas of discussion and thought and prayer. Some groups make use of pubs as meeting places, others may find a restaurant more appropriate, at least occasionally.

(iv) Using men

Identifying and making use of gifts and skills helps men to be valued and appreciated. This does not just mean repairing the church roof. Some men have great organisational skills; others may be gifted speakers and could be encouraged in speaking, teaching and evangelism. After all, if you are putting on a course to discuss work and Christianity the Vicar isn't going to be the only leader, or even the leader at all—is he?

(v) Teaching children

Caring for the children of the church family is a responsibility men need to share in. Some churches are making specific efforts to involve men in leading groups for children, if necessary releasing them from other tasks. Also in relation to that, several churches have set up parallel boys and girls groups from roughly age 10 upwards. This seems to be helping in retaining boys at the time they often drift away from the church. Their needs are another whole area for discussion.

(vi) Social events

Church social events can be aimed at the whole family and be planned with men in mind. For example, one church organized an All Saints Party as an alternative to Hallowe'en. There was a rolling programme from 6 p.m. to past midnight. Men were specifically involved in the planning and running of the children's events and part of the evening consisted of a cheese and wine party for adults able to attend. It finished with a time of intercession and communion.

(vii) Church services

Men are used in leading services but ask how a man coming for the first time will react. Will he easily find his way through the book or follow at least the main changes of posture? Is he asked to sing embarrassing words? Asking the questions will keep us more open to new men.

The final word on this is a reminder not to take on too much too soon. In prayer and discussion seek God's way forward and set realistic targets. The first and biggest step is simply greater awareness of men's needs within the activities of the church.[1]

3 The Future—Evangelism and Growth

As we move from discipling church-going men to evangelising those outside a great gulf appears. On their own admission, according to a recent survey,[2] 92% of men do not go to church weekly. We have already examined many of the causes and indicated some ways the local church can change its ways. To help us cope with thinking about this vast sea of irregular attenders and non-attenders I have used the categories of the church growth movement. Evangelistic methods and ideas are described in each category, though, as always, there is overlap.

Different writers use different terms. The ones that follow are taken from *How Do Churches Grow?* by Roy Pointer. He describes the four types of growth[3] as internal, expansion, extension and bridging.

... (a) Internal Growth

This is evangelizing nominal Christians already attending church, calling them to re-dedication to Jesus. It includes the teaching of children of believers, bringing them to an adult commitment as they grow up. It is effectively what is described in Section 2 above and may not lead directly to numerical growth. Indeed, it can lower the number of attenders as greater emphasis is put on the demands of discipleship.

... (b) Expansion Growth

This mostly results from the addition of unbelievers who are of a similar culture to those already in the church. The task here is to remove what Pointer calls the 'stained-glass' barrier. As far as men are concerned it means relating what goes on in church activities to the rest of their lives. It means using language and actions appropriate to the culture, and not allowing them to fossilize. If we use house groups—and they are one of the most potent means of growth—it is important that their formats are suitable. We may need men-only groups, or groups for shift workers, the unemployed, or those involved in particular kinds of work. The aim here would not be to isolate such men but to give them a place in which to find their Christian feet.

---

[1] These examples come from my own enquiries and from *A Man's Life Workbook* (CPAS), a workbook with a video training package of the same name, and from *The Way to a Man's Heart* (Administry Resource Paper 85:6).
[2] MARPLAN Poll reported in *Church Times*, 12 December 1986.
[3] *op. cit.,* pp.150-156.

It is this type of numerical growth which is easiest to achieve. 'Like attracts like' when it comes to joining a group. As you would expect, most of the ideas tried in the evangelism of men have been of this type. Of the methods mentioned some are more strictly described as pre-evangelistic, breaking the ground, but that does not stop God using them to convert men sometimes.

'Agnostics Anonymous'—'An opportunity to discuss matters of religious significance with no holds barred'. How do you square a God of love with so much suffering and evil in the world'?—'All religions lead the same way'.—These groups have been used successfully in missions to men. I have used them with invitations to men and women and found men more ready to come. Their value lies in breaking down at least some misconceptions and in building up relationships with Christian men. They also provide Christian men with the chance to share their faith in a new way. Individual invitations are a great help.

A variant of this idea has been held by a church, also in an area with a large proportion of professional men. In this case the meeting was a one-off on a Saturday, with a stimulating speaker. The intention was to make a 'pub-like' atmosphere—but one in which the men would talk about more serious issues. An important point was keeping the number of non-Christian men higher than the Christian. Conversation flowed, though conversions have not yet. The main visible results have been in deepening the faith of Christian men and in building good relationships within the community.

A house church in a more working class setting has also tried to build friendships as a first step towards conversion. In their case it has been through shared activities such as snooker-playing and working together.

A problem area for some meetings is that of music. For some groups singing is still fine, but many unchurched men are unaccustomed and embarrassed by it—watch them at the next wedding or funeral you attend. In some places a straight lecture with questions and answers can be the solution.

The evangelist, Eric Delve, frequently finds as many men as women responding to his presentation. His belief is that it is the presentation of Jesus that is important, and the church is seen as those determined to follow him whatever the cost. It is not an appeal to purported masculine strength. It is a recognition that men have a 'funny mixture of pride and conscious weakness.'[1] His encouragement is that it is possible to see men converted as we share our vision of Jesus.

The meetings and events in section 2 are all potentially evangelistic. If you have a men's group going of any kind should some of its regular meetings be specifically evangelistic? The use of pubs is often particularly useful here because they are seen as neutral ground, even by infrequent pubgoers. Jim Smith gives some helpful guidelines.[2] The main point is to

[1] Personal communication from Eric Delve, 5 November 1987.
[2] *Manhunt,* p.142f.

choose a speaker able to cope with pub dynamics. The other things to watch for are consideration for the landlord—let him know what you are doing, check the room, have food available.

These events and more are described in *Manhunt* and *A Man's Life Workbook*. However, it is important to see them as part of a bigger strategy. These work on a time-scale of a year or two ahead and can be freshened up regularly.

In format, at least, they work within their cultures, though they are different from the prevailing church culture. As we move on to the next form of growth we see existing church culture challenged more strongly and begin to challenge contemporary society more.

. . . (c) Extension growth

This still involves people of a similar culture to the evangelizing church but they are joined to a new congregation. This area of church-planting is widely agreed to be absolutely crucial to major growth but is also being widely neglected in this country.[1] This has particular benefits for reaching men with drive because it provides new openings for leadership. A good example of this happening occurred when Holy Trinity, Brompton, planted a congregation in a redundant building. It has the advantages of being able to start without so much cultural baggage as the sponsoring church, of being able to be flexible in its initial structures, and of breaking new ground in assumptions about meeting times and places.

Nor is it necessary to envisage a costly building programme: there are several alternatives. These include the use of private homes, existing church halls and other premises such as schools and social clubs, and, as at least one church is trying, the use of one building but at different times of the day.[2]

This method has been widely used amongst house churches and found to be of great benefit. It is worth commenting here that insofar as I have been able to find out they have fairly good female/male ratios. One of the main reasons I believe lies in this kind of growing and splitting structure. An additional factor might be the emphasis many put on male leadership; however, there are big variations between different churches on this issue. These variations do not seem to be reflected in their female/male ratios.[3]

. . . (d) Bridging growth

This is cross-cultural church planting. There will be variations within this between cultures closer to the church's own and those further away. In

[1] See the forthcoming Grove Booklet on Evangelism work: Gavin Reid (ed.) Bob Hopkins *Church Planting* (November 1988).

[2] See also Ian Bunting's chapter in *Hope for the Church of England?* (Kingsway, 1986). He describes the growth of separate congregations within a parish, away from the parish church. Ken Gardiner *Watch This Space*, pp.146-9 indicates some of the problems and benefits.

[3] This area does warrant further investigation, especially for those who fear that women priests would mean a worsening female/male ratio in the Church of England. Could it be that women leaders can bring out qualities and responsibilities in men which other men find it harder to do?